For Elodie, Finn, and Eyck,

who are traveling so fast

through their childhoods,

and for Shirley Foo,

who has helped us all through.

Book design by Elizabeth B. Parisi   •   Photography by Saxton Freymann & Nimkin/Parrinello

Library of Congress Cataloging-in-Publication Data Available

ISBN 0-439-11019-X

10 9 8 7 6 5 4 3 2 1   06 07 08 09 10

Printed in Singapore 46 • First edition, March 2006

Fast Food

Written and Illustrated by Saxton Freymann

🏮 ARTHUR A. LEVINE BOOKS

An Imprint of Scholastic Inc. / New York

Your feet can walk
and run
and skip.

But are they best for every trip?

With skates, a walk becomes a glide.
A skateboard can extend your stride.
Need something you can hold on to?
A scooter might be right for you.

If you cannot walk about,

a wheelchair's here to help you out.

Pedal hard aboard a bike.
Add a wheel, and it's a trike!

Down snowy hills,
you'll need some skis.
Bundle up so
you don't sneeze!

Ice skates are for crossing ice,

but on the snow, a sleigh is nice.

Sometimes you'll want to travel far.
Maybe then you'll choose a car.

It might be wise if more of us would ride together...

...in a bus!

If you have heavy
loads to haul,

a truck will
help you
move them all.

A fire truck speeds toward a fire,
full of heroes who inspire.

But fire trucks can't hesitate!
When sirens wail, please stop and wait.

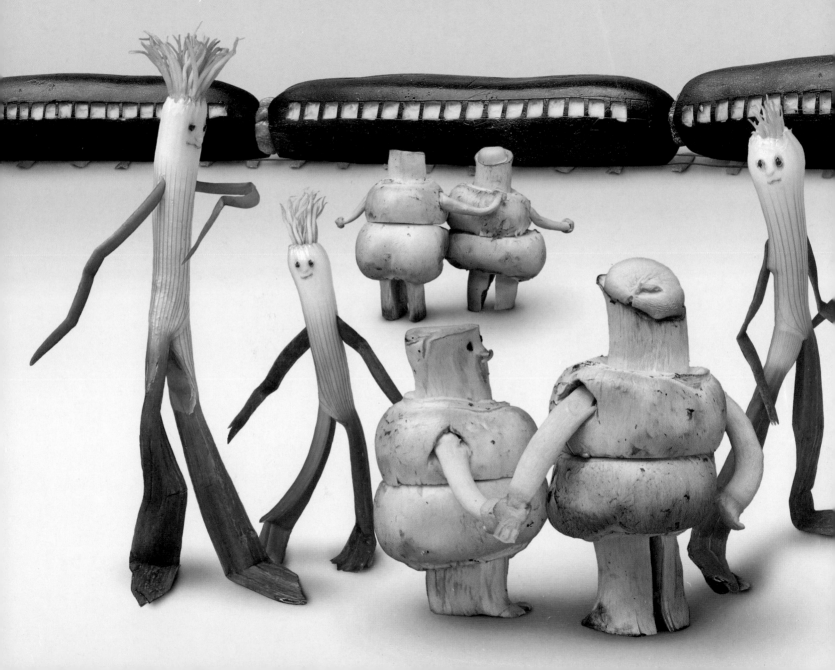

Trains speed along, click clack, click clack,

to all the stations on the track.

On water it is best to float,
so climb aboard your favorite boat.

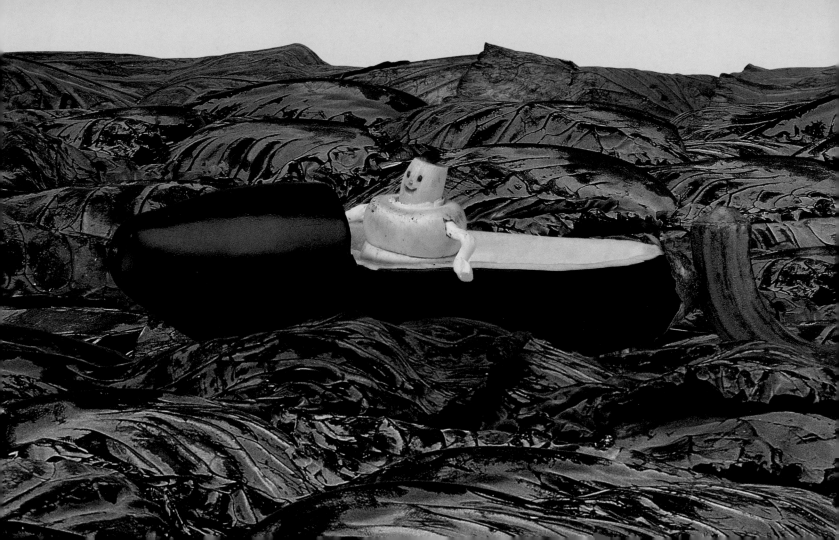

Some move by motors, some by rowing...

...some only when the wind is blowing.

If there's no rush, there's nothing finer
than cruising on an ocean liner.

Want to see the ocean floor?
A submarine lets you explore.

To travel far and fast, you fly
in an airplane through the sky.

A helicopter chops the air.
It hovers and lands anywhere.

Go by blimp or by balloon,

or take a rocket past the moon!

By foot, on wheels, by air or sea,
I hope that soon you'll visit me!